Mind Over Me

Tammy L. Malone

Copyright © 2011 Tammy L. Malone

All rights reserved.

ISBN: 145638211X
ISBN-13: 9781456382117
LCCN: 2010917666

I dedicate this book

To my family of life, with whom I have shared these experiences

✧ ✧

Contents

1. Reflective Pond Pg. 1
2. Cacti Pg. 5
3. Path to Nowhere Pg. 11
4. Shining Through Pg. 17
5. Calm Lake Side Pg. 23
6. By the Sea Pg. 31
7. White Blossoms Pg. 37
8. Behind the Grass at the Sea Pg. 43
9. Broken Tree on the Lake Pg. 51
10. An Old Bridge Pg. 57
11. Bright Blue Sky Pg. 63

Chapter One

REFLECTIVE POND

Tammy L. Malone

Writing

Poetry and prose
Words among my mind just so
Looks of question upon my face
Sense of it all, I try to make
The words start to flow
To paper and pen I must go
The words pour like rain
I must write as fast as a train

If I wait too long
My words are gone
And I must wait
For the words to take

These words tell my story
They show my pain
And they show my joy
From one time or more

As Time Goes By

every day is closer to the future
              ...every second
              ...every minute
as time passes by it seems sometimes slow
sometimes fast
years have come and gone so quickly
i just sit and think about where it all went
time waits for nothing
              ...it just keeps ticking away
sooner or later
              the future
will become
              the present
              ...and time will have past me by

Chapter Two

Cacti

He Says:

There's no reason not to love him in some way
There's no reason for me to feel this way
I should have the answers to his questions, anyway
I should know why I feel this way

He can no longer live this way
He doesn't understand why I feel this way
I just keep moving further away
I should know why I feel this way

His words seem to shut me down in some way
He says I'm not normal, I'm not right all the way
He thinks I'm crazy and should be put away
What he doesn't realize is he made me this way

Our Love

The nights that we shared
The days filled with glare

Each hour of time that goes by
I'm wishing you weren't at my side

When I'm thinking of you
It's hard not to cry

The love that we shared
Will not always satisfy

Bitter

the bitter taste of a red rose
a reflection of their souls
dance like a supple kiss
in the rain of a soft mist
the slip of words cannot be unspoken
unanswered questions are so broken
eyes of brown tearing down her cheek
her physical being is so meek
the clouds of white, the clouds of gray
her emotional being has been stolen away
the love that binds them has been worn
tension lies heavy all the more
forgotten memories and hopeless dreams
the emptiness of her heart seems serene
through the memories they shared
their hearts were seldom there
love flickers like a candle in the wind
and like the shore line does ripple

Chapter Three

Path to Nowhere

Alone

I reached a point in my life
That left me feeling weak
Unwanted emotionally
My days were life of routine
Left alone
In a house, not a home
Two healthy boys
With minds of their own
Depression came upon me
Sleep is all I wanted to do
Where there were no problems
No responsibility
And no more feeling alone

I'm Just A Dreamer

I want…
To live in a small town
With open meadows
And trees swaying in the breeze
…I'm just a dreamer

I want…
To own a house
With a white picket fence
And a swing hanging in a tree
…I'm just a dreamer

I want…
To be by the seaside
With the waves at my feet
And the suns warmth on my face
…I'm just a dreamer

I want…
Money in my pocket
To spend as I need
And to drive where ever I please
…I'm just a dreamer

Butterflies

Swinging, swinging
So far above the grounds
I'm suspended in the air

Butterflies, butterflies
The words come in mounds
But the feeling is quite clear

Scary, scary
I can't hear any sounds
All I can do is just stare

I'm suspended in the air
The feeling is quite clear
And all I do is just stare

Untitled

Though you have never walked on this earth
There isn't a time that goes by
That I don't think of you
I am always in search of your name
Even though I couldn't give you birth
I hope you can forgive me
Although I, myself, find it hard to

Chapter Four

Shining Through

Her Presence

Her Spirit
I felt her here
Next to me one night
I forced her away
Scared, in a calm way, you see

I wanted her to stay
But I didn't know how
To respond to her being here
I hope she's always near
Even though her presence is not clear

A Visitor

The curtains are blowing
But the windows are closed

The walls are closing in
And the floor is quickly sinking

The ceiling is no helping kind
While chills run up my spine

Take my hand
I hear her whisper

A light comes on
Much too bright

Now she is gone
Swallowed in the light

No more whisper
No more hand to take

My Angel

I have Angels all around me
Flying high and flying low
Sitting beside me
And singing soft and low

My Angel rubs my back
While I sleep and while I nap
My Angel kisses my tears away
Morning, noon and night

My Angel lets me know when near
Whispering in my ear, I hear
The sounds of comfort and joy
I see my Angel's smile so coy

My Angel knows what I'm thinking
Right by me without ever blinking
My Angel is in my heart and mind
Her ways with me are so kind

My Angel saves my life
Keeps me breathing all the night
Lets me wake in the morning light
I'm glad to have my angel's sight

Chapter Five

Calm Lake Side

My Marine

A man stands before me
In his fatigues
With a rifle in hand
He is my Marine, this man

He fights for me
For me to walk down the street
To drive in my car
And to fly in a plane

A husband, a father, stands before me
He sacrificed, do they know that of he
He has to leave them behind
When will he see them again in time

A friend stands before me
Laughing, joking, and having fun, you see
We hope we will have that again before long
I wish we could go back there, for now so long

My brother stands before me
In his Dress Blues so neat
His face shows hard
He stares right threw me, with his guard

He has seen others die
Die beside him, behind him, and he says good bye
I could not imagine, day or night
What he has seen, in his fight

Mind Over Me

I am so proud of him
Proud of whom he has become
Proud of his being
And proud to be his sister

A man stands before me
A friend stands before me
My brother stands before me
He is my marine — My Marine

My Wish to You

May happiness always follow you
Wherever you may go to
May your sorrows be quick to lose
Whenever they come to you

May all your dreams come true
And nightmares stay away from you
For your dreams may all come true
But your nightmares will always haunt you

To Lisa

To Lisa,
my lifelong friend,
and to Roger,
her love of life,
and my newfound friend...

Through all that life has to offer,
there are many highs
to keep our heads in the sky.
And as we all know,
many low moments
to bring us to our knees.

Everyday
we can learn more about ourselves
as well as everyone around us.

Make your life together
as special as it can be.
Listen to each other
even if what is being said
is not spoken in words.

Never lose communication
with one another.
Treat each other as an equal
being, as one together
has more power
than one's power alone.
Passion
can be stronger than words.
But remember to always say,
"I Love You."

From the bottom of my heart
    to both of yours,
        with all my love,
           always

A Note to A Friend

A friend is a friend,
Someone you would do anything for.

Someone you would risk your life for,
Give anything for.

Friendship and love, is it all in one?
Does it mean the same?

          I think so!

A lifetime of friends
Would not add up
To a lifetime of a friend as you.

A magical time,
Maybe a fantasy so,
But it's true to my heart,

          A friend as you!

My Love Will Always Grow

Love is like a dream of clouds
Dancing up above so loud.
As beautiful as the smell of a rose
Blooming so red across the cove.

Love may come and go,
But my love for you will always grow.

Chapter Six

BY THE SEA

Tammy L. Malone

Waves

The wave of sound
Crashing along the shore
Sharp and cold
And burying my feet
Just to be swept
Back into the sea
Disappearing to no end
But soon again will be seen

Mind Over Me

Cluster of Trees

One leans against another
As if its' head on ones shoulder
Looking for support
From one so strong

So straight and tall
It's reaching, reaching high
As if to say I am strong
So lean on me and bring me your sorrow

The Mirth of Spring

Mother Nature's painting of serene expression
Grounds magically coming alive with resilient color
The sounds of birds chirping, the harmony of bubbling creeks
Fragrant flowers, freshly cut grass,
Beaches of warm sun, soft sand under my feet
Sand castles of creativity, a seaward gaze
Children flooding the parks; bikes, skates, basketball, Frisbee
Bees that sting
Secret kisses in the meadow
Moonlit walks with the soft touch of another's hand
The feel of an evening breeze

> Sweet love
> Blue skies
> White linen clouds
> Wings of birds in flight
> Daylight stretched in time
> Simple dress, wet glistening skin
> So far away, far from me
> Noiselessly, with no words
> Blazing red flame of sun
> The days burn in my mind
> I am a stranger
> Taken down
> Waiting…
> …darkening sky, sun set…Waiting
> …waiting for the sun to rise

Feels Like

sleeping on a cloud and floating like an angel

crying in the rain and growing like a tree

riding in the wind and flying like a bird

shining like the sun and blooming like flowers

bathing in the sea and swimming like a fish

singing with the thunder and shining like lightning

Chapter Seven

WHITE BLOSSOMS

The Most Beautiful Thing

I've heard people say
That the best part of living
Is dying
I have never understood that statement
Until recently
I had a conversation with someone
Who had a near death experience
And she told me,
"It was the most beautiful thing
You will ever see…
It was the most wonderful feeling
That will ever come upon you"
I hope this person realizes
How much that conversation means to me
It helped me with a family death
And I have to believe
She could not resist death
That she accepted death
That she accepted the journey
To the heavens above
I have to believe
That she did see
The most beautiful thing
She could have ever seen…

Mind Over Me

A Eulogy

I started to cry the instant I heard
For so long my tears, like rain poured
I will miss your hugs, your kisses, your smile,
Your laughter the most

We cried many tears
Embraced in our hugs
We laughed until our eyes watered
And our cheeks hurt

I will miss your warmth, your smile,
Your laughter the most

To all of us here
She is your sister, your once wife, your mother,
Your very special friend too,
Our Aunt, a great Aunt, a cousin to a few,
A wonderful friend, a neighbor, and an acquaintance to you

I will miss your warmth, your smile,
Your laughter the most

To one,
"Friendship Café" was your home
Where all the seats were taken
And now, there will always be an empty one

To us all,
Memories flashed before our face
Our hearts pounding at a faster pace
You will be remembered
And in time our feelings we will mend

I will miss your warmth, your smile,
Your laughter the most

Tammy L. Malone

I know A Place

I know a place
Way up high
Where the angels sing
With whispers of lullabies
Where the rain never falls
And the night is always bright

I know a place
Way up high
Where the clouds like cotton
Are under my feet
Where the thunder and lightening
Never do meet

I know a place
Way up high
Like sugar and honey
That are more than just sweet
Where the bees do not sting
And nothing does weep

I know a place
Way up high
Where soft wings cradle me tight
And where all I see
Are rainbows of flowers
Blooming morning until night

Chapter Eight

BEHIND THE GRASS AT THE SEA

Tammy L. Malone

No Escape

Echoing sounds of their yelling,
Thundering sounds of things breaking.
To the attic I go, in crawl space I stay.
Where, for a short time, I pray.
Frightened? Not here, anyway.
Trapped in the drapes, up upon the sill.
Fists pounding, I cannot escape.
Stolen I was; he took us away.
He stole my innocence, nothing more to say.
Frightened? Yes, nowhere else to stay.
My childhood was brushed away.
Not to be spoken in any way.
Frightened…I have no emotion, just a body I say.
Now years have gone by…
Frightened? Not anymore, I am raged!

Shadow in the Dark

She sits in the corner
Her eyes rain down her cheeks
Her cries are not heard
She feels out of place

She sits in the corner
Her eyes rain down her cheeks
She feels she isn't seen
Like a shadow in the dark

She sits in the corner
Her eyes rain down her cheeks
She is physically in the world
But not seen in the light

Waiting

I have been away
From myself for so long
That my body just breathes
And I only move to the beat of life

My mind has taken control
And I am just waiting
For life to pass me by
Since no one knows how to help

As a mother and a wife
I would be missed
But mentally and emotionally
I am not here to any further extent

I need the rain
To wash me away
I've hid within myself
Tired of living life

Maybe I'll fall asleep
And never wake

A Sleepless Night

The cool breeze passes over my skin
I hear the leaves of the highest trees
The sounds of crickets I can hear too
Another sleepless night in this world

How do I change my world with the fewest of tears?

I need to flourish, to create,
And to smile again
Every second of every day
I want to be happy with more in my life

How do I find compassion and comfort in my heart?

An embracing hug that feels right
So right it cannot be put into words
Wishing for a tender kiss
Another sleepless night in this world

How can I feel alive again?

My state of mind; not usually a happy time
No emotion, no feeling at all
All that surrounds me is standing still
Except the dancing shadows made by the moon

How can I sleep tonight?

The cool breeze passes over my skin
I hear the leaves of the highest trees
The sounds of crickets I can hear too
Another sleepless night in this world

Tammy L. Malone

The Attic is Where I Like to Be

A line divides your yard and mine
We can play together
Without saying a word
We can get by
With just hi and bye

It's time for me to go
Home to the other side
Where harsh words are always spoken
Where I have no emotion
As soon as I walk in the door

Too many of us
For such a small house
Sharing a bedroom, sharing a bed too
Always turmoil and cluttered and loud
The attic is where I like to stow

A crawl space in the attic
Is where I like to be
Insulation and sawdust
The smell relaxes me so
I could sit here forever and just be removed

Chapter Nine

BROKEN TREE ON THE LAKE

Tammy L. Malone

While in My Youth

Did you ever think
While growing up
That life would be
So difficult
Financially
Emotionally
And physically too
Not many smiles
No laughter heard
Tears just fall
With sleepless nights
I wish that life
Was as I dreamt
While in my youth

My Grandmother's Ring

A symbol of their love, my grandmother's ring
A diamond encased in a box setting of gold
A cross, two raised, to protect them so
She has left to me this ring
Its shank is worn and so thin
I'm wearing my Grandmother's ring

Tammy L. Malone

Another Breath

I always thought
That I was afraid
Of my death one day

Now I know
It's not death itself
Just not another breath to take

I'm still afraid
Of my death one day
So I don't want to know
When I have not, another breath to take

Untitled

The wind blows
And their shadows
Dance all around

The room is empty
But the ceiling
Walls and floor

No Color
To speak of
I stand alone

Chapter Ten

An Old Bridge

A Present

In this box you will find
A memory that was left behind.

It brought you pleasure both night and day,
But somewhere in time it slipped away.

Over time you learn through your heart
That what once was so small can still play a big part.

So open your heart and let your mind go
To a place where your memory can grow.

Love Always,

Written on a Christmas present to me by my Aunt Pat in 1997. Inside…Mrs. Beasley…

Grammy's Untitled

Why can't I make you see
how much
you have become a part of me?
It's been so long
since we've been together.
Those special moments,
I'll always remember.
It hurts so much
to know you don't care.
The pain in my heart
is hard to bear.

Written by my grandmother,
Waneta Alderson (Brown) Stevens,
sometime in the early 1970's.

So Alone

Another night has gone by,
I'm trying so hard not to cry.
Without you,

I'm so alone;
No more calls on the phone,
No more secret meetings,
To worry about your cheating.

I'll always remember,
What we shared,
And how you cared.

Our love was so strong,
It couldn't have been wrong.
You always held me tight,
Making everything all right.

Your lips so tender,
When we kissed.
I hope you know,
How much you're missed.

I'm trying so hard,
To understand,
Why God took you,
To another land.

*Written by my grandmother,
Waneta Alderson (Brown) Stevens,
sometime in the early 1970's.*

Mind Over Me

With You I'd be Strong

You asked me
To help you to be strong.
Why?
Is what we felt really so wrong?
When we are together,
Or either of us call,
You make me feel
Like I'm ten feet tall.
What little we have shared
Is heavenly bliss.
I dream of your body,
Your caress, your kiss.
The look in your eyes,
The warmth of your touch,
I know in your heart,
You want me as much.
I've tried so hard
To reach out for help,
But you cannot or will not
Give yourself.
I'm so alone,
How can I go on
Weak, like I am?
With you I'd be strong!

*Written by my grandmother,
Waneta Alderson (Brown) Stevens,
sometime in the early 1970's.*

Chapter Eleven

Bright Blue Sky

A Special Place

Welcoming hellos
Paintings and drawings line the walls
Bright colors perform all around
Music entertaining the surround
Soothing as a spring brook trickling by
Pottery of shape displayed along the isle
Relaxing as lavender lingering by your nose
The atmosphere is poetry and prose
Start with your favorite herbal tea
With sweet desserts on your taste buds indeed
Hope you enjoyed, see you again soon please

My Sisters...My Brother,

Sisters are a gift, nothing else can compare, except for a brother who we all think is dear.

When we were young we sure filled a house. We fought, we yelled, we pushed and shoved, who really cared?

My memories for the most part are clear. Sometimes I felt sad, lonely and scared, other times I felt happy, very cared for and grateful. Most of all I felt loved! Of course we all owe that to Mom...she cared.

Now that we are older, thank God we are all still here. We all get wrapped up in our own little worlds. We all have our own families, friends and careers...cheers!

With all this comes some sadness from the worries, stress and fears.

My sisters, my brother...when we all come together I feel so much laughter, comfort and joy but most of all I feel loved! I only wish for more togetherness each and every year.

Because of all of you, I always had someone to love and I always felt loved.

Thank you all for being so loving, kind and dear,

Your loving sister, Tina
Sincerely...I care

Written by my sister, Tina Marie (DeCoito) O'Connor

About The Author

I am 44 years of age and ready to put this book of poems to print. The words written upon these pages are of my most personal thoughts, feelings, and life experiences as I see them. Some of these poems date back to my teen years. I had found at a young age that paper and pen are my best friends. I feel that time does heal; I have learned to forgive, but I have not forgotten.